ANANIAS FOR ONE ANOTHER

Opening Prayer: A Lectio with Acts 9 :10-19

Follow these simple steps for your opening prayer:

1. Say a brief prayer. Invite the Holy Spirit to open your eyes and ears to what God has to say to you today through His Word.

2. One person reads the passage aloud. Allow for a moment of silence after the reading is complete.

3. Make note of any word or phrase that stands out to you in this passage.

4. As another person reads the passage, listen for your chosen word or phrase. Allow some time for silence : What is the Lord saying to you today through His Word?

5. Close with a prayer of thanksgiving for the opportunity to hear God speak through his Word today.

6. Share with your partner(s) what stood out for you in this passage.

There was a disciple in Damascus named Ananias, and the Lord said to him in a vision, "Ananias." He answered, "Here I am, Lord."

The Lord said to him, "Get up and go to the street called Straight and ask at the house of Judas for a man from Tarsus named Saul. He is there praying, and [in a vision] he has seen a man named Ananias come in and lay [his] hands on him, that he may regain his sight."

But Ananias replied, "Lord, I have heard from many sources about this man, what evil things he has done to your holy ones in Jerusalem. And here he has authority from the chief priests to imprison all who call upon your name."

But the Lord said to him, "Go, for this man is a chosen instrument of mine to carry my name before Gentiles, kings, and Israelites, and I will show him what he will have to suffer for my name."

So Ananias went and entered the house; laying his hands on him, he said, "Saul, my brother, the Lord has sent me, Jesus who appeared to you on the way by which you came, that you may regain your sight and be filled with the holy Spirit."

Immediately things like scales fell from his eyes and he regained his sight. He got up and was baptized, and when he had eaten, he recovered his strength. —Acts 9:10-19

WHO WAS ANANIAS?

In Acts 9:10, the Lord appears to Ananias of Damascus in a vision and lays upon him a difficult task: minister to Saul, a known persecutor of Christians and an accomplice to the stoning of St. Stephen. Yet Ananias says "yes"—despite his fears—and agrees to meet Saul.

Other than a brief mention in St. Paul's conversion testimony in Acts 22, there is no further mention of St. Ananias of Damascus in the Bible. However, his willingness to be an instrument of God's grace at a key moment in the conversion of St. Paul was a game changer, for St. Paul and for the Church.

Catholic tradition holds that Ananias was eventually martyred in the Holy Land. On the world stage, by secular standards, Ananias played a bit part. However, it is a lesson for all of us that God can do great things with small acts of love and obedience on the part of his disciples.

Ananias and Saul: with the disciples in Damascus

After three days in Damascus, Saul met Ananias. The scales fell from his eyes and he was baptized. Ananias, however, was not some guru or lone ranger. He was part of a community of disciples in Damascus. The Acts of the Apostles goes on to recount that Saul stayed with the disciples in Damascus for "some days", proclaiming Jesus as the Messiah in the synagogues (Acts 9:19b-20).

We don't know what was said between Ananias and Saul. We also do not know exactly how the community helped Paul become a disciple. We do know this: Jesus did not leave Saul alone after his initial encounter with him (Acts 9:10-19), and Paul grew strong in this community of disciples in Damascus (Acts 9:22).

BREAKING THE SILENCE:
BEING ANANIAS FOR ONE ANOTHER

Much as Saul came to understand his encounter with Christ during his "days with the disciples in Damascus" (Acts 9: 20), in today's Church, we come to a deeper relationship with God and a deeper understanding of our call to follow Jesus in a community of fellow believers.

Sherry Weddell, in her book, *Forming Intentional Disciples,* describes the need to break the culture of silence present in many Catholic communities: a culture in which it is not normal to talk about one's relationship with Jesus Christ (pp. 189-190). Being an "Ananias" for one another as we journey to follow Jesus can transform this culture of silence, replacing it with a culture in which having a personal relationship with Jesus Christ and following him in the midst of his Church is normal. The fruit of a culture of discipleship is that more people are attracted to the community, and come to encounter Jesus themselves.

The story of Ananias as instrument of God's mercy and provision in the life of St. Paul is a story told and retold, lived and relived, throughout the centuries. For example, St. Monica and St.

Ambrose accompanied St. Augustine on his journey of conversion and discipleship. For St. Elizabeth Ann Seton, the Filicchi family were among many who accompanied her as she journeyed toward the Catholic Church and went on to found the first American religious community for women, the Sisters of Charity.

> From Evangelii Gaudium:
>
> "The Church which "goes forth" is a community of missionary disciples who take the first step, who are involved and supportive, who bear fruit and rejoice." "...Missionary disciples accompany missionary disciples."

Pope Francis in *Evangelii Gaudium,* describes the importance of journeying alongside others in order to grow in our relationship with Christ:

"In a culture paradoxically suffering from anonymity and at the same time obsessed with the details of other people's lives, shamelessly given over to morbid curiosity, the Church must look more closely and sympathetically at others whenever necessary.

In our world, ordained ministers and other pastoral workers can make present the fragrance of Christ's closeness and his personal gaze. The Church will have to initiate everyone – priests, religious and laity – into this "art of accompaniment" which teaches us to remove our sandals before the sacred ground of the other (cf. Ex 3:5). The pace of this accompaniment must be steady and reassuring, reflecting our closeness and our compassionate gaze which also heals, liberates and encourages growth in the Christian life. Although it sounds obvious, spiritual accompaniment must lead others ever closer to God, in whom we attain true freedom." (169-170)[1]

This is something within the reach of **all** who follow Jesus. Modern-day "Ananiases" are at work in our communities today, helping people encounter Jesus, allowing them to be transformed by that encounter, and/or walking with them as they begin the journey of intentional discipleship. They are priests, religious and lay, and live in our homes, towns and workplaces as parents, siblings, spouses, friends, co-workers, and neighbors.

What does it mean to you to know you are called to journey alongside your brothers and sisters in Christ as an Ananias?

What does it mean for you to know that you are called to become a missionary disciple? And that you are not alone in that call?

What gifts do you think God has given you to be an Ananias for others? What tools do you think you still need?

Listening with the Ears of the Heart

"We need to practice the art of listening, which is more than simply hearing. Listening, in communication, is an openness of heart which makes possible that closeness without which genuine spiritual encounter cannot occur. Listening helps us to find the right gesture and word which shows that we are more than simply bystanders. Only through such respectful and compassionate listening can we enter on the paths of true growth and awaken a yearning for the Christian ideal: the desire to respond fully to God's love and to bring to fruition what he has sown in our lives."

—Pope Francis, Evangelii Gaudium, 171

1 - To read more about what Pope Francis has to say about spiritual accompaniment, read Evangelii Gaudium, 169-173. You can find it online here: http://w2.vatican.va/content/francesco/en/apost_exhortations/documents/papafrancesco_esortazione-ap_20131124_evangelii-gaudium.html

BEING A GOOD LISTENER

Here are some suggestions on how to be a good listener:

Tip #1: *Pray*

Take a moment to remind yourself you are in the presence of God.

Ask for the Holy Spirit's guidance

If the other person is open, pray with them

Tip #2: *Be Fully Present*

This is a good time to disconnect from all electronic devices and other distractions in order to be fully present to the person in front of you.

Tip #3: *Listen to Every Word*

Tip #4: *Be a Reflective Listener (think "mirror")*

Summarize what they have shared ("What I heard you say was,...")

Tip #5: *Ask Clarifying Questions*

Can you tell more about … ?

What happened next?

Why do you think … ?

Tip #6: *Yield Not to Temptation...*

To advise, teach, counsel, or in any way don a "fix-it" hat.

We listen and respond in order to guide them in discovering for themselves how God is present in their life.

Tip #7: *Self-Disclosure—Rare and Brief*

Keep the focus on the other.

If you do share something about yourself, ask a question to return the focus to them.

Tip #8: *Know When to Refer Out*

Your ministry leader or parish staff can provide you with guidance in this area.

NEVER ACCEPT A LABEL IN PLACE OF A STORY

Paul was an older gentleman, called upon by the RCIA team to sponsor another older gentleman preparing to become Catholic. Paul was a very faithful Catholic, active in the men's ministry, hot foods ministry, and a member of the Pastoral Council. By all outward measures, everyone assumed he was close to Jesus.

At the first gathering with the newly baptized after Easter, Paul stood up, leaned on his cane, and began to share what happened to *him* during RCIA. He said he always came to Mass with the idea that somewhere, on some divine score card, he had checked another box assuring him entry into Heaven—what he called his "fire insurance." "During these sessions," he went on to say, "I met Jesus. I mean, I really met Jesus, *for the first time. And I decided it was high time that I become his disciple.*"

Paul's testimony stunned everyone in the room. For all presumed that Paul must have been a disciple, in a personal relationship with Jesus. Why else would he be so active and committed to his parish?

Paul's story is a good reminder that how someone describes themself (such as, "practicing," "devout" or even "fallen-away" Catholic) is not enough to know where they are in their lived relationship with God. Only in hearing their story can we begin to understand their relationship with God.

In other words, we should be wary of accepting labels in place of stories.

THREE SPIRITUAL JOURNEYS

...Communion with Jesus, which gives rise to the communion of Christians among themselves, is an indispensable condition for bearing fruit: "Apart from me you can do nothing" (Jn 15:5). And communion with others is the most magnificent fruit that the branches can give: in fact, it is the gift of Christ and His Spirit...

*...Through evangelization the Church is built up into a **community of faith**: more precisely, into a community that **confesses** the faith in full adherence to the Word of God which is **celebrated** in the Sacraments, and **lived** in charity, the principle of Christian moral existence. In fact, the "good news" is directed to stirring a person to a conversion of heart and life and a clinging to Jesus Christ as Lord and Saviour; to disposing a person to receive Baptism and the Eucharist and to strengthen a person in the prospect and realization of new life according to the Spirit...*

— St. John Paul II, *Christifideles Laici*

For the intentional disciple, following Jesus in the midst of His Church encompasses three spiritual journeys.[2]

1. **The personal interior journey of lived relationship with Christ, resulting in intentional discipleship.**
   [Jesus said,] "I am the vine, you are the branches. Whoever remains in me and I in him will bear much fruit, because without me you can do nothing." —John 15:5
   As we live the life of an intentional disciple, we are called to a deeper relationship with Jesus. Our ability to undertake our mission fruitfully rests upon the attention we give to this relationship.

2. **The ecclesial journey into the Church through reception of the sacraments of initiation.**
   For in one Spirit we were all baptized into one body, whether Jews or Greeks, slaves or free persons, and we were all given to drink of one Spirit. —1 Corinthians 12:13

2 Forming Intentional Disciples, 54-55

Christian initiation is accomplished by three sacraments together: Baptism, which is the beginning of new life; Confirmation which is its strengthening; and the Eucharist which nourishes the disciple with Christ's Body and Blood for his transformation in Christ.

—Catechism of the Catholic Church, 1275

Through the sacraments of Baptism, Confirmation and Eucharist, we are joined with Christ and oriented toward eternal life with Him. Through the outpouring of the Holy Spirit, we also receive charisms which equip us to live out our unique vocation as a disciple of Jesus.

3. **The journey of active or inactive practice (as evidenced by receiving the sacraments, attending Mass, and participating in the life and mission of the Christian community.)**

They devoted themselves to the teaching of the apostles and to the communal life, to the breaking of the bread and to the prayers. Awe came upon everyone, and many wonders and signs were done through the apostles. —Acts of the Apostles 2:42-43

Go, therefore, and make disciples of all nations, baptizing them in the name of the Father, and of the Son, and of the holy Spirit, teaching them to observe all that I have commanded you. And behold, I am with you always, until the end of the age." —Matthew 28:19-20

When we participate in the life of the parish, not only is the community strengthened but we grow closer to Jesus and begin to discover how we are called to participate in His Mission.

CLOSING PRAYER

Sign of the Cross

Leader: As we conclude this time together, let us ask for the intercession of the Blessed Virgin Mary as we pray:

Reader One: Mary, Virgin and Mother, you who, moved by the Holy Spirit, welcomed the word of life in the depths of your humble faith as you gave yourself completely to the Eternal One, help us to say our own "yes" to the urgent call, as pressing as ever, to proclaim the good news of Jesus.

Reader Two: Filled with Christ's presence, you brought joy to John the Baptist, making him exult in the womb of his mother. Brimming over with joy, you sang of the great things done by God.

Reader Three: Standing at the foot of the cross with unyielding faith, you received the joyful comfort of the resurrection, and joined the disciples in awaiting the Spirit so that the evangelizing Church might be born.

Reader Four: Obtain for us now a new ardor born of the resurrection, that we may bring to all the Gospel of life which triumphs over death.

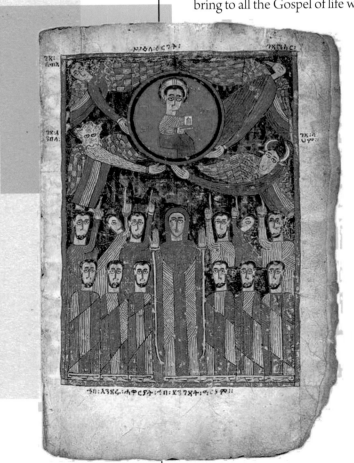

Reader One: Give us a holy courage to seek new paths, that the gift of unfading beauty may reach every man and woman.

Reader Two: Virgin of listening and contemplation, Mother of love, Bride of the eternal wedding feast, pray for the Church, whose pure icon you are, that she may never be closed in on herself or lose her passion for establishing God's kingdom.

Reader Three: Star of the new evangelization, help us to bear radiant witness to communion, service, ardent and generous faith, justice and love of the poor, that the joy of the Gospel may reach to the ends of the earth, illuminating even the fringes of our world.

Reader Four: Mother of the living Gospel, wellspring of happiness for God's little ones, pray for us.

All: Amen. Alleluia!

—Pope Francis, *Evangelii Gaudium*

NO TWO JOURNEYS THE SAME

Opening Prayer

He had to pass through Samaria. So he came to a town of Samaria called Sychar, near the plot of land that Jacob had given to his son Joseph.

Jacob's well was there. Jesus, tired from his journey, sat down there at the well. It was about noon. A woman of Samaria came to draw water.

Jesus said to her, "Give me a drink." His disciples had gone into the town to buy food.

The Samaritan woman said to him, "How can you, a Jew, ask me, a Samaritan woman, for a drink?" (For Jews use nothing in common with Samaritans.)

Jesus answered and said to her, "If you knew the gift of God and who is saying to you, 'Give me a drink,' you would have asked him and he would have given you living water."

[The woman] said to him, "Sir, you do not even have a bucket and the cistern is deep; where then can you get this living water? Are you greater than our father Jacob, who gave us this cistern and drank from it himself with his children and his flocks?"

Jesus answered and said to her, "Everyone who drinks this water will be thirsty again; but whoever drinks the water I shall give will never thirst; the water I shall give will become in him a spring of water welling up to eternal life."

The woman said to him, "Sir, give me this water, so that I may not be thirsty or have to keep coming here to draw water."

Jesus said to her, "Go call your husband and come back."

The woman answered and said to him, "I do not have a husband." Jesus answered her, "You are right in saying, 'I do not have a husband.' For you have had five husbands, and the one you have now is not your husband. What you have said is true."

The woman said to him, "Sir, I can see that you are a prophet. Our ancestors worshiped on this mountain; but you people say that the place to worship is in Jerusalem."

Jesus said to her, "Believe me, woman, the hour is coming when you will worship the Father neither on this mountain nor in Jerusalem. You people worship what you do not understand; we worship what we understand, because salvation is from the Jews. But the hour is coming, and is now here, when true worshipers will worship the Father in Spirit and truth; and indeed the Father seeks such people to worship him. God is Spirit, and those who worship him must worship in Spirit and truth."

The woman said to him, "I know that the Messiah is coming, the one called the Anointed; when he comes, he will tell us everything."

Jesus said to her, "I am he, the one who is speaking with you."

At that moment his disciples returned, and were amazed that he was talking with a woman, but still no one said, "What are you looking for?" or "Why are you talking with her?"

THRESHOLDS OF CONVERSION

Chapters 5-8, FID

Pre-Discipleship

Focus: Lived Relationship with God, Baptized or unbaptized, churched or unchurched

1. Initial Trust

2. Spiritual Curiosity

3. Spiritual Openness

4. Spiritual Seeking

5. Intentional Discipleship

The woman left her water jar and went into the town and said to the people, "Come see a man who told me everything I have done. Could he possibly be the Messiah?"

They went out of the town and came to him.

Many of the Samaritans of that town began to believe in him because of the word of the woman who testified, "He told me everything I have done." When the Samaritans came to him, they invited him to stay with them; and he stayed there two days. Many more began to believe in him because of his word, and they said to the woman, "We no longer believe because of your word; for we have heard for ourselves, and we know that this is truly the savior of the world." —John 4:4-30; 39-42

- As you listened to this story, what part of the Samaritan woman's story strikes you?

- What part best fits with your own relationship with Jesus right now?

Recall: Pre-Discipleship Spiritual Development

- God's grace is present and active in the early stages of spiritual development that are **not intentional discipleship.**

- No two people respond in the same way to God's grace.

- We need to hear where they have been in order to respond effectively to people at different points in their journey.

- Never accept a "label" in place of a "story."

CROSSING THRESHOLDS

Always remember:

Thresholds will look different to those who are not yet disciples than they will for disciples or church insiders.

We are not in control. Some people are not yet ready to respond to an invitation to follow Jesus.

How we respond can cause people to stall in their journey or move back to an earlier threshold.

From non-believing, non-trusting to Trust

A woman of Samaria came to draw water.

Jesus said to her, "Give me a drink."

"How can you, a Jew, ask me, a Samaritan woman, for a drink?" (For Jews use nothing in common with Samaritans.)

What have been the "bridges of trust" (persons, places, things) along your own journey?

Non-believing, non-trusting

Trust – threshold 1:
of Christ, the Church, the faith, a Christian

Baptism

Christ

Pre-evangelization – preparing people for first proclamation of the Gospel

HAVE YOU BEEN PART OF A BRIDGE OF TRUST IN ANOTHER PERSON'S JOURNEY?

Second Threshold: Curiosity

"Everyone who drinks this water will be thirsty again; but whoever drinks the water I shall give will never thirst; the water I shall give will become in him a spring of water welling up to eternal life."

The woman said to him, "Sir, give me this water, so that I may not be thirsty or have to keep coming here to draw water."

*"The first and most obvious question is 'Curiosity about what?' The answer is that if our ultimate mission is to make disciples of Jesus Christ, our task at this stage in the journey is to first arouse curiosity about **Jesus Christ**. To do that we have to **talk about Jesus**."* –FID, 141

Spiritual Curiosity...

… involves trust, but does not imply real openness to change. Not yet.

… is a passive threshold. One who appears curious may not yet be actively seeking.

… is a "natural" tendency and can be intentionally fostered.

… is a place where those who don't believe in a God with whom you can have a personal relationship can explore that possibility at this threshold.

… needs a safe, non-threatening space in which people can express their curiosity without over- reaction or pressure from us.

Stages of Curiosity

Awareness. There are more possibilities than I had imagined or have experienced.

Engagement. I am willing to take some baby steps on my own: making friends with a Christian, reading about Jesus, watching a video online, etc.

Exchange. This is a stage of intense curiosity: not just listening but actively asking questions and exchanging ideas. The focus of curiosity: a relationship with Jesus is possible—for some but not necessarily for me personally… yet.

SPIRITUAL OPENNESS

Remember: Openness…

… is not discipleship. **It is a tentative openness to God and the possibility of spiritual change**.

… is still essentially passive.

You may not be *certain* that you can have a personal relationship with God, but must be open to the possibility.

Moving from curiosity to openness is one of the hardest transitions to make.

You must lower your defenses (cynicism, antagonism), and acknowledge to God (if He is really there and listening!) and yourself that you are open to change. It can feel dangerous, crazy, horrific, out of control.

Jesus said to her, "Go call your husband and come back." The woman answered and said to him, "I do not have a husband."

Spiritual Seeking: "Dating with a Purpose"

"I know that the Messiah is coming, the one called the Anointed; when he comes, he will tell us everything."

Remember, Seekers Seek Jesus!

Not just God in a general sense or the "divine" or an "impersonal force".

Seeking is active: intentionally exploring relationship with Christ and his Church and the possibility of discipleship.

It is not yet intentional discipleship. But it does require certainty that a personal relationship with God is possible because that is what you are exploring. (It's dating with a purpose, not marriage).

Those who are "open" don't always want to come to a conclusion.

Seekers intentionally seek resolution. They want to connect the dots. "I need to make a decision."

Becoming a seeker may not look that different on the outside, but can feel dramatically different to the one on the journey. There is an urgency. It feels like a quest.

One cannot remain a seeker forever: there is a sense of urgency, of "I have to make a decision or forget the whole thing."

Seekers count the cost. *This is the place where they begin to grapple with the sense of personal sin.*

We can especially help people at this stage by answering their questions, praying with, and praying for them.

INTENTIONAL DISCIPLESHIP

Jesus said to her,

"I am he, the one who is speaking with you."

The woman left her water jar and went into the town and said to the people,

"Come see a man who told me everything I have done. Could he possibly be the Messiah?"

The decision:
To follow Jesus in the midst of His Church

"This conversion is the acceptance of a personal relationship with Christ, a sincere adherence to him, and a willingness to conform one's life to his.

Conversion to Christ involves making a genuine commitment to him and a personal decision to follow him as his disciple."
National Directory for Catechesis, p. 47-48

DISCIPLES TELL THEIR STORIES!

Many of the Samaritans of that town began to believe in him because of the word of the woman who testified, "He told me everything I have done."

Note:

The Journey to Becoming an Intentional Disciple

… is different for every person.

… is often not a straight line to becoming a disciple.

… can have many twists and turns.

… can go in reverse at certain points in our lives.

… can stall in one place: for days, weeks, months, even years.

TRACE YOUR OWN JOURNEY

A reading:

Jesus said to his disciples; "I am the true vine, and my Father is the vine grower. He takes away every branch in me that does not bear fruit, and everyone that does he prunes so that it bears more fruit. You are already pruned because of the word that I spoke to you. Remain in me, as I remain in you. Just as a branch cannot bear fruit on its own unless it remains on the vine, so neither can you unless you remain in me. I am the vine, you are the branches. Whoever remains in me and I in him will bear much fruit, because without me you can do nothing. Anyone who does not remain in me will be thrown out like a branch and wither; people will gather them and throw them into a fire and they will be burned. If you remain in me and my words remain in you, ask for whatever you want and it will be done for you. By this is my Father glorified, that you bear much fruit and become my disciples." – John 15:1-8

In the time provided, trace your own spiritual journey through the thresholds. Our journeys are often full of twists and turns: there is no "right" journey just "your journey."

Some questions that may aid your reflection:

1. Look at the five thresholds diagram on the next page. To draw a line showing your journey through the thresholds <u>to this point</u> in your life, begin by marking the following on the diagram:

Beginning from your earliest memories of your relationship with Jesus, at what threshold were you:

- at specific life milestones: school graduation, work, retirement, marriage, birth of children, serious illness, death of a love one, divorce;

- when you first received the sacraments of Baptism, Reconciliation, Confirmation?

Note your age by each point you where you crossed a threshold (either going toward or away from Jesus)

2. Trace a path connecting your marks in chronological order.

Some questions:

- What precipitated your crossing each of the thresholds? Traumatic or joyful events? Important people? Books? A change in your environment? Add those to the diagram.

- At what threshold are you now? How long have you been there?

- Where would you like to be?

- What needs to change in your life to get there?

- What obstacles (internal/external) to a deeper relationship with Jesus exist that you need to overcome with his grace?

- Who and/or what is sustaining you in your relationship with Jesus at this time?

After you have completed this exercise, please turn to the page 18.

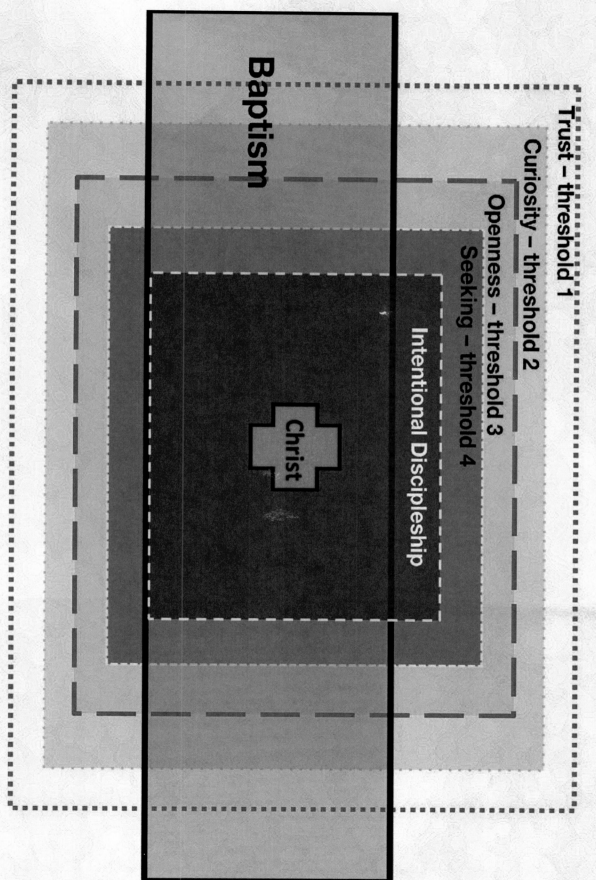

Baptism

Trust – threshold 1

Curiosity – threshold 2

Openness – threshold 3

Seeking – threshold 4

Intentional Discipleship

Christ

Non-believing, non-trusting

Preparing to Hand Over Your Life to Jesus Before the People of God

As part of our retreat experience you will be given an opportunity to participate in a prayer ritual that will connect you with your Baptism. During this ritual you will be given an opportunity to hand over your whole life to Jesus.

In preparation for this ritual, ask the Holy Spirit to give you a word that encapsulates what giving your life over to Jesus means for you.

Once that word is given to you, return to the main prayer space carrying that word in your heart.

As part of the ritual you will be asked to say that word out loud before the People of God. Our prayer will conclude by praying the Angelus together.

NOTE: *If you are completing this ritual on your own, you may want to pray the Prayer of St. Ignatius of Loyola, on the bottom of page 19, after you say your word aloud.*

Handing over our whole lives is a process. At this time in your life you might find yourself feeling not ready to make this type of decision. This ritual is an opportunity to hand over your life to Jesus. It is also an opportunity to tell Jesus that perhaps you are not ready but are open to growing to the point of making that decision.

The Angelus:

L(eft Side):The Angel of the Lord declared to Mary:

R(ight Side): And she conceived of the Holy Spirit.

Hail Mary...

L: Behold the handmaid of the Lord:

R: Be it done unto me according to Thy word.

Hail Mary . . .

L: And the Word was made Flesh.   R: And dwelt among us.

Hail Mary . . .

L: Pray for us, O Holy Mother of God,

R: that we may be made worthy of the promises of Christ.

Leader: Let us pray:

All: Pour forth, we beseech Thee, O Lord, Thy grace into our hearts; that we, to whom the incarnation of Christ, Thy Son, was made known by the message of an angel, may by His Passion and Cross be brought to the glory of His Resurrection, through the same Christ Our Lord. Amen.

A Mystagogy: Listening & Sharing—in Groups of 3 to 4

Without going into too much detail, describe briefly what the "word" you used in the prayer ritual means for you.

What was the prayer ritual experience like for you?

After her encounter with Jesus, the Samaritan woman returned to her village to tell the people what had happened. To whom are you sent? Friends, family, parish? How is God calling you?

Do you have a sense of what gifts you have received through baptism and confirmation that Jesus calls you to use in proclaiming the Kingdom of God?

THOUGHTS

Prayer of St. Ignatius of Loyola

Take, Lord, and receive all my liberty,
my memory, my understanding,
and my entire will,
all I have and call my own.

You have given all to me.

To you, Lord, I return it.
Everything is yours; do with it what you will.
Give me only your love and your grace, that
is enough for me.

DO CHAT : HAVING A (THRESHOLD) CONVERSATION

Opening Prayer

***Lectio Divina:* The Rich Young Man and Jesus** *Instructions are found on page 57 of this manual.*

As he was setting out on a journey, a man ran up, knelt down before him, and asked him, "Good teacher, what must I do to inherit eternal life?"

Jesus answered him, "Why do you call me good? No one is good but God alone.

You know the commandments: 'You shall not kill; you shall not commit adultery; you shall not steal; you shall not bear false witness; you shall not defraud; honor your father and your mother.'"

He replied and said to him, "Teacher, all of these I have observed from my youth."

Jesus, looking at him, loved him and said to him, "You are lacking in one thing. Go, sell what you have, and give to [the] poor and you will have treasure in heaven; then come, follow me."

At that statement his face fell, and he went away sad, for he had many possessions.

—**Mark 10:17-22**

Think of a friend, family member, co-worker, or someone perhaps you know from church:

WHAT QUESTIONS WOULD THEY HAVE FOR JESUS?

WHAT OBSTACLES MIGHT KEEP THEM FROM SAYING "YES" TO JESUS?

Threshold Conversations: The Basics

Adapted from "Guide for Threshold Conversations" ©2010, Sherry Weddell. Used with permission.

A Threshold conversation is intended:

…To *invite an individual to talk,*

… Simply and directly *about one's lived relationship or journey with God,*

…While we listen respectfully and prayerfully, *seeking to learn what spiritual threshold one may have reached.*

The purpose of a Threshold Conversation: To know where and how to start encouraging another to make the next step on the journey toward intentional discipleship.

A Threshold Conversation *is*	A Threshold Conversation is NOT:
• Prayerful	• Spiritual Direction
• Respectful	• Faith sharing
• Companionable	• Apologetics
• Supportive	• Catechesis
• Friendly, inviting	• Interrogation
• Open-ended	• Judgmental

With whom can I have a threshold conversation?

You can have a threshold conversation with anyone: friend, co-worker, neighbor, family member, fellow parishioner, acquaintance provided trust has been established.

How long is a threshold conversation?

A threshold conversation can be as long or as short as necessary to fit the situation. You can "drop in" and "drop out" of a threshold conversation as circumstances dictate.

Where can one of these conversations happen?

Threshold conversations can happen anywhere you encounter someone desiring to talk, such as:

- over lunch or coffee at a local diner
- at a kitchen or dining room table
- over the fence with a neighbor
- waiting in line at a store or supermarket
- on the sidelines of a soccer field
- after Mass, over coffee and donuts

- someone in RCIA, preparing to become Catholic
- couples preparing for marriage
- confirmation candidates
- school or religious education parents
- returning Catholic

REMEMBER

Simply *asking* this question and really *listening* to the answer <u>can change lives</u>.

Never accept a label in place of hearing a description of the other's lived experience of God. *Always* ask what he means by the label of "atheist" or "agnostic" or "Catholic" or "spiritual".

Listen for "Seeds of the Word" —ways God has prepared this person to hear the good news of Jesus Christ and his Church.

We listen at *multiple levels.*

Beginning a Threshold Conversation

The question:
Can you describe your relationship with God to this point in your life

8 KEY LISTENING POINTS

- Believe in God?
- What *kind* of God? (personal or impersonal)
- Believe in *possibility of relationship* with this God?
- Have a *relationship with this God*? What *kind of relationship*?
- Part of a *religious tradition*? What tradition?
- *Points of trust* re: Christ, Church, faith, a Christian?
- Knowledge of/lived relationship with *Jesus Christ*?
- Christian? Intentional Disciple? Apostle?

How to know where a Threshold Conversation should go[3]

FOR THOSE WHO RESPOND ...

- "I don't believe in God."

- "I don't know if there is a God."

- I believe in a "Higher Power" or "Impersonal Force."

OUR FOCUS SHOULD PROBABLY BE ON:

- *Building and nourishing trust* and/or

- *Fostering curiosity* about a God with whom you can have a personal relationship.

> *For more on how to respond to #1-3, see Section "A", pp. 25-27.*

FOR THOSE WHO RESPOND:

- "I believe in personal God but don't have a relationship to respond to an invitation to follow Jesus.

OUR FOCUS SHOULD PROBABLY BE ON:

- *Building and nourishing trust* and/or

- *Fostering curiosity* about the possibility of a personal relationship with God through Christ and/or

- Helping her *become open to possibility of spiritual change and personal relationship with Christ.*

> *For more on how to respond to #4, see section "B", p.28.*

For those who respond:

5a. "I believe in a personal God but am unaffiliated with any faith community."

5b. "I believe in a personal God and am affiliated with a non-Christian faith."

5c. "I believe in Jesus, but don't consider myself a Christian."

OUR FOCUS SHOULD PROBABLY BE ON:

* *Building and nourishing trust* and/or

* *Fostering curiosity* about the possibility of a *personal relationship with God through Christ*

  and/or

* Helping her become *open to spiritual change and personal relationship with Christ*

  and/or

* Encouraging serious seeking, wrestling with the *possibility of following Christ in the midst of his Church as a intentional disciple*

For further guidance regarding responses 5a-5c, see section "C", pp. 28-30.

For those who respond:

5d. "I have a relationship with a personal God and consider myself a Christian but seldom or never go to church".

5e. "I have a relationship with a personal God and am an 'active' Christian (but don't seem to be a disciple)."

OUR FOCUS SHOULD PROBABLY BE ON:

* *Building* and nourishing *trust* **in Christ and his Church**

  and/or

* Helping her become *open to spiritual change and personal relationship* **with Christ and his Church**

* Encouraging serious *seeking*, wrestling with the *possibility of following of Christ in the midst of his Church as an intentional disciple*

  and/or

* Challenging him to 'drop the net" and *become an intentional disciple.*

For further guidance regarding responses 5d-5e, see section "D", pp. 30-31.

SECTION A

1. Self-Description: "Atheist" or "I don't believe in God".

When someone describes himself as an "atheist", he may *not* mean that he doesn't believe in any God at all. *He may be trying to say that he doesn't believe in a particular version or description of God.*

ASK PEOPLE WHO DESCRIBE THEMSELVES AS "ATHEISTS"

- What do you mean by "atheist?"

- Tell me about the God you don't believe in.

- Sum up his description of the God he doesn't believe in. Then ask:

    Do you believe in any other kind of God or universal spirit?

If he says "**yes**", ask: ***Can you describe the God you do believe in?*** Take the conversation in the direction that matches his response. (*See sections B, C, D, pp. 28-31*)

If he says "**no**": take the conversation in the *"I don't believe in God"* direction below.

THE "I DON'T BELIEVE IN GOD" CONVERSATION:

Possible Spiritual thresholds: non-trust, trust, curiosity

Suggested clarifying questions:

- Have you ever believed in God? If so, why did you stop?

- Do you ever pray? If so, how?

- What gives meaning to your life?

- Have you had any significant exposure to religion or spirituality? Ever attended a religious congregation or school?

- Are you close to any religious or spiritual person(s)? Why do you like/trust him or her? What role does God play in their life? How do you feel about that?

(If it seems appropriate)

Could you ever imagine believing in God? If so, what would that God be like?

If he seems to be at threshold of curiosity, ask:

What do you know or believe about Jesus Christ?

REMEMBER: "ATHEISTS" CAN BE SURPRISINGLY RELIGIOUS!

- **15%** believe in God or a "universal spirit"

- **6%** believe in a God with whom you can have a relationship

- **19%** are formal members of religious congregations

- **14%** attend religious services at least yearly

- **5%** are involved in congregational activities monthly

- **10%** pray at least weekly outside religious services

- **21%** believe miracles happen today

- **39%** have talked to other people about their ideas of God (so they may well be open to talking to you!

Pew Religious Landscape Survey, 2008

2. Self-Description: "Agnostic" or "I don't know"

ASK "AGNOSTICS":

- What do you mean by 'Agnostic'?

- Do you believe in a God or universal spirit?

If she says "yes", ask: *Can you describe the God you do believe in?* Take the conversation in the direction that matches her response. (See sections B, C, D, pp. 28-31.)

If she says *"I'm not sure"* or *"I don't know"*, take the conversation in the *"I'm not certain"* direction below:

"AGNOSTICS" CAN BE EVEN MORE SURPRISING!

- **40%** believe in God, only 16% 'don't know'.

- **14%** believe in a God with whom you can have a relationship.

- **22%** are formal members of religious congregations.

- **18%** attend religious services every month/year.

- **5%** are involved in congregational activities monthly.

- **18%** pray at least weekly outside religious services.

- **37%** believe miracles happen today.

- **36%** have talked to other people about their ideas of God. *(so they may well be open to talking to you!)*

Pew Religious Landscape Survey, 2008

THE "I DON'T KNOW/I'M NOT CERTAIN" CONVERSATION:

Possible Spiritual thresholds: non-trust, trust, curiosity

Suggested clarifying questions:

- Have you always been uncertain? If not, what caused you to become uncertain?

- What difference would it make to you if you could be sure God existed? If God existed, what do you think he would be like?

- If a God like that existed, would you want a relationship wit that God?

- Do you ever pray? If you do, describe when and how you pray.

- What gives meaning to your life?

- Have you had any significant exposure to religion or spirituality at some point? Ever attended a religious congregation or school?

- Are you close to any religious or spiritual person(s). Why do you like or trust him or her?

- What role does God play in their life?

- How do you feel about that?

If she is at threshold of curiosity, ask:

What do you know or believe about Jesus Christ?

3. Self-Description: "I believe in God"

We cannot assume that he means a "personal" God with whom a human being can have a relationship. **Always** ask him about the kind of God he believes in.

If he indicates he believes in a personal God, take the conversation in the direction that matches his response. *(See sections B, C, D pp. 28-31)*

If he indicates he believes in a "*Higher Power*" or "*Impersonal Force*", take the conversation in the direction below.

THE "I BELIEVE IN A HIGHER POWER/ IMPERSONAL FORCE" CONVERSATION:

Possible spiritual thresholds: pre-trust, trust, curiosity

Suggested clarifying questions:

- How would you describe the Power you believe in?

- What do you call the Power?

- What difference does this Power make in your life?

- Do you ever pray? If so, how?

- Are you part of any religious or spiritual community?

- If so, how is your involvement with that faith community related to your belief in the "Higher Power"?

- Are you close to any religious or spiritual person(s). Why do you like or trust him or her?

- What role does God play in their life? How do you feel about that?

If he seems to be at the threshold of curiosity, ask:
What do you know or believe about Jesus Christ?

REMEMBER: WHEN SOMEONE SAYS "I BELIEVE IN GOD," WE STILL DON'T KNOW WHAT KIND OF GOD HE BELIEVES IN

Many people believe "God" is an **"impersonal force."**

- **29%** of Catholics

- **12%** of atheists

- **36%** of agnostics

- **40%** of "secular unaffiliated"

- **35%** of "religious unaffiliated"

- **19%** of Protestants

- **34%** of Orthodox

- **50%** of Jews

Pew Religious Landscape Survey, 2008

SECTION B

4. Self-Description : "I believe in a personal God *but don't have a relationship with that God.*"

THE "I BELIEVE IN A PERSONAL GOD, NO RELATIONSHIP" CONVERSATION:

Possible Spiritual thresholds: *non-trust, trust, curiosity, openness*

Suggested clarifying questions:

- Could you describe the God you believe in?

- Why don't you consider yourself to have a relationship with God? If you thought it was possible to have a relationship with God, would you want one? Why or why not?

- Have you attended or are you part of a particular religious or spiritual community? If so, which one(s)?

- Do you ever pray? If so, how?

- Are you close to any religious or spiritual person(s)? Why do you like or trust him or her? What role does God play in their life? How do you feel about that?

- What gives meaning to your life?

If she seems to be at the threshold of curiosity or openness, ask:
What do you know or believe about Jesus Christ?

SECTION C

5. Self-Description: I believe in a personal God *with whom I have a relationship*

We may need to ask another question here (if he doesn't volunteer this information):

Q: Are you part of a particular religious faith or community? Depending upon the answer, take the conversation in the following directions:

- ***No.*** *Not part of any religious faith or community, "unaffiliated".* **Go to page 29, 5a.**

If the answer is **"Yes", take the conversation in one of these directions:**

- ***Yes.*** *Non-Christian faith.* Which one? **Go to page 29, 5b.**

- ***Yes.*** *"Believe in Jesus" but not a Christian.* **Go to page 30, 5c.**

- ***Yes.*** *Personal Christian faith, "unchurched", not active.* **Go to page 30, 5d**

- ***Yes.*** *Personal Christian faith, active member of a Christian community.* **Go to page 31, 5e.** Which one? Intentional disciple? Apostle?

5A. THE "I HAVE A RELATIONSHIP WITH A PERSONAL GOD BUT AM UNAFFILIATED WITH ANY FAITH TRADITION" CONVERSATION.

Possible Spiritual Thresholds: *non-trust, trust, curiosity, openness, seeking*

Suggested clarifying questions:

- How important is your relationship with God now? Was there an important turning point in your relationship with God? What has deepened your relationship with God? Why?

- Do you pray? If so, when and how do you pray?

- Have you ever been part of a religious community or tradition?

- If yes, did your involvement with that community or tradition foster your relationship with God?

- How?

- Why are you no longer involved?

- Are you open to being part of a religious tradition or community again at some point? What would make you want to do that?

If she seems to be at the threshold of curiosity, openness, or seeking ask:

What do you know or believe about Jesus Christ?

5B. THE "I HAVE A RELATIONSHIP WITH A PERSONAL GOD AND AM PART OF A NON- CHRISTIAN FAITH TRADITION" CONVERSATION

Possible Spiritual Thresholds: *non-trust, trust, curiosity, openness, seeking*

Suggested clarifying questions:

- What religious community or tradition do you belong to?

- How would you describe your relationship with God?

- How important is your relationship with God now?

- Was there an important turning point in your relationship with God?

- Has your involvement with your faith community nourished your relationship with God?

- How?

- Has anything else helped to deepen your relationship with God? How?

- Do you pray? If so, when and how do you pray?

- How active are you in your faith community?

If he/she seems to be at threshold of curiosity, openness, or seeking ask:

What do you know or believe about Jesus Christ?

5c. The "I believe in Jesus but I'm not a Christian" Conversation

Possible Spiritual Thresholds: *non-trust regarding the Church and Christianity, trust, curiosity, seeking*

Suggested clarifying questions:

- How would you describe your relationship with Jesus today?

- How did you first encounter Jesus? Was there an important turning point in your relationship with Jesus? What has deepened your relationship with Jesus? Why?

- Do you pray? When and how do you pray?

- Why do you consider yourself not to be a Christian? Were you a Christian at one time? If so, what happened to change that? Do you think that you might ever be a Christian in the future?

- Have you ever attended or been part of a Christian church or community? If so, which one(s)? Have you been baptized? Have your received some kind of Christian education or catechesis?

- Have you ever attended or been part of a non-Christian religious community? Which one(s)?

SECTION D

5d. The "I am a believing Christian but seldom or never attend church" Conversation.

Possible Spiritual Thresholds: *non-trust regarding the Church or Christians as a community, trust, curiosity, openness, seeking, intentional disciple*

Suggested clarifying questions:

- How would you describe your relationship with God today? Do you have a relationship with Jesus? Describe it.

- How did you first encounter Jesus? Was there an important turning point in your relationship with Jesus? What activities, relationships, or resources most nourish your relationship with Christ?

- Do you pray? If so, how?

- Have you ever been part of a church or Christian community?

- If yes, did your involvement with that community or church foster your relationship with Christ?

- How?

- Why are you no longer involved?

- Are you open to being part of a church or Christian community again at some point?

- What would make you want to be an active part of a local church?

5E. THE "I HAVE A PERSONAL CHRISTIAN FAITH AND AM ACTIVE IN THE CHRISTIAN COMMUNITY" CONVERSATION.

Remember to listen for signs of intentional discipleship and/or apostleship.

Possible Spiritual Thresholds: *curiosity, openness, seeking, intentional disciple?*

Suggested clarifying questions:

- How would you describe your relationship with God today? Do you have a relationship with Jesus? Describe it.

- How did you first encounter Jesus? Was there an important turning point in your relationship with Jesus? What activities, relationships, or resources most nourish your relationship with Christ?

- Do you pray? If so, describe when and how you pray.

- Do you presently attend church regularly? Which one(s)? Have you been baptized? Are you ivolved in church activities beside Sunday services? Which ones?

- How do you express your faith (besides attending church) at this point in your life? In your relationships/family? In your job/workplace? In your community? In your volunteer activities? In your recreation?

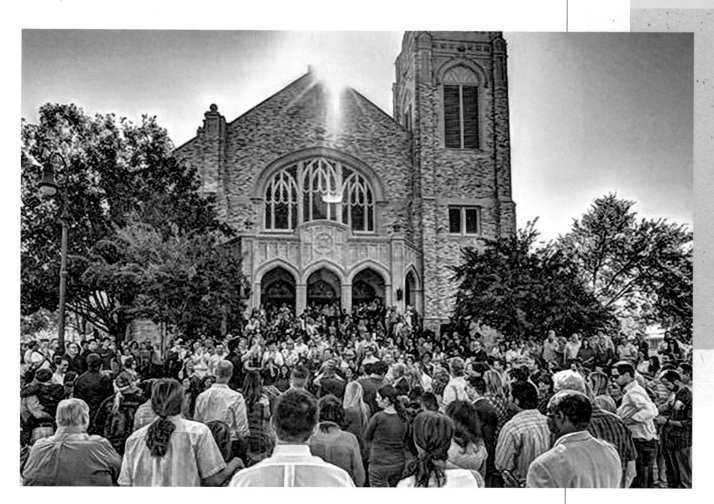

How to Bring a Conversation to a Close...

One possible way to end a threshold conversation, if the other person **really trusts** you or you are in a formal pastoral setting, is with this question:

"If you could ask God one question that you knew He would answer right away, what would it be?"

- The answer will usually reflect some of his current questions, struggles; felt needs.

- You may be able to address the needs that arise yourself, depending upon your relationship with this individual and the need that emerges.

- If not, do you know some person who might be able to help or an appropriate resource in the parish ordiocese?

IF YOU CAN HELP, PLEASE DO SO — but outside a ministry context. It usually isn't your responsibility to have the answers. It is your job to be a friend who understands and can be an informal spiritual companion.

THIS IS A GREAT QUESTION

1. ...to ask people considering becoming Catholic as you can structure the inquiry period around their burning personal questions.

2. ...to ask parents of teens, elementary-age students in the parish school or religious education program in order to identify their spiritual needs.

REMEMBER that during a threshold conversation, you are not doing faith-sharing, catechesis or apologetics.

IF POSSIBLE, instead of answering questions, answer briefly and then ask a question in return that invites them to share more of their story. You can drop in and out of short threshold conversations (5 or 10 minutes) quite naturally in the midst of a longer conversation with a friend, colleague, or family member. What matters is the content of the conversation, the fact that you really listened and asked good questions, and that he trusts you enough to talk to you about something this personal.

FOCUS FIRST on understanding his journey and asking clarifying or curiosity-inducing questions, *not* primarily on answering factual questions about the Christian faith. Don't let sharing information get in the way of hearing his story.

A THRESHOLD CONVERSATION could take 5 minutes or an hour or more. Don't try to prolong the spiritual conversation when the other person chooses to change the subject. Pray quietly, entrust the fruit of the conversation to God, and relax. Some people move to a new threshold just through telling their story! You and the Holy Spirit may have set the stage for further conversations in the future!

ON THE VERGE OF INTENTIONAL DISCIPLESHIP?

What if you are listening deeply to a person share their story, and you sense that, perhaps, this individual is on the verge of intentional discipleship? Perhaps you feel a holy nudge from the Holy Spirit, to invite this person to respond to Jesus' invitation … *now.*

This can happen in many different places and often is an unexpected surprise!

First, take a deep breath and ask God to guide your thoughts and your words. Then, reflect upon what you have heard, and perhaps know from previous conversations, about this person's story.

What we need to discern in that moment is: Is this person truly ready to follow Jesus, or is this merely a reflection of our own desire for them?

Here are some clues to look for in their conversation that can guide your discernment:

They have begun to make some changes in their life, such as:

- Praying daily
- Reading scripture
- Spending time with believers, some of whom may already be disciples. This may be in:
     Work settings
     Social settings
     At parish events, or part of a parish ministry
- Recognizing, and repenting of, their own personal sin
- Making changes in their life that address sinful and/or unhealthy behaviors
- Wrestling with being part of the Church—attending Mass, or other parish events
- And … asking questions about "next steps"

They are asking you questions, such as:

- How did you come to be a disciple of Jesus?
- Why do you do *X*?
- How did you change your priorities?
- Why is following Jesus important to you?
- Isn't following Jesus enough? Why do you: spend time at the parish, go to Mass, go to Bible study, confession, serve in ministry, etc.
- What would I need to do to follow Jesus?
- How do I: become part of the parish, receive Communion, be baptized, etc.?

Suppose there are several of these clues evident in this person's story.

- *How do you invite them to respond and "drop their nets"?*
- Second, recognize that you might be wrong … they may be moving in that direction but not as far along as you think. Therefore, how we invite them to respond to Jesus' invitation needs to leave open the possibility of responding, "*no, not yet.*"

How to invite someone to "drop their nets"

Sometimes it is very clear that all that is needed is to simply ask, "Would you like to follow Jesus?"

Often, individuals need some context to understand why we are asking the question so that it is not a total surprise. In those situations, it helps play back to them what we have heard in the conversation that prompts us to ask, such as:

"While I was listening to you share "x", I had a strong sense that Jesus was inviting you to become his follower. Can I help you say yes to Jesus' invitation to be his disciple today?"

If he/she says yes, lead them in a prayer. Here are some suggestions:

Pray together:

- Help this person say yes to Jesus' invitation to follow him as his disciple

- Thank God for the gift of their yes, and a continued openness to being his disciple

- Pray that he or she be open to the grace to live out this yes everyday

- If it is appropriate, pray before the Blessed Sacrament.

If you are this individual's sponsor for Baptism or Confirmation, you may want to be prepared to pray together the Creed, or lead them in a renewal of baptismal promises. Your parish leader can show you how to do this.

If he/she is already a baptized Christian, this is a simple way to help them renew the promises of their baptism:

- Do you believe that God the Father created you and loves you?

- Do you believe that Jesus, God's only son, came to earth, suffered, died and rose from the dead to free you?

- Do you acknowledge your sins and ask God to forgive your sins, so that you can be truly free?

- Do you want to follow Jesus as his disciple?

If he/she says "yes", your work is not done! Following Jesus takes a different set of spiritual muscles than seeking. Therefore, new disciples need an Ananias more than ever in those early weeks, as they learn a new way of living and growing in their relationship with God.

Here are some things you can do to help new disciples:

- Be present. Listen to them as they share their stories of newfound life with Jesus.

- Introduce them to other disciples. Invite them to spend time with them.

- It is especially helpful for them to meet individuals who have been disciples for less than a year. New disciples can tell stories that connect to their newfound relationship with Jesus, helping them as they learn and grow.

- Spend time doing "disciple things" together:

    Pray together

    Read the Bible together

    Go to Mass together

    Serve together

- Help them encounter the Church

    Introduce them to potential disciple-friends. Helping them find a small community of disciple-friends can be helpful.

    If they desire baptism, confirmation, and or First Communion, connect them with the people at the parish who can assist them. Go with them, if you can, as they make the ecclesial journey.

    If you can, go with them to Mass and various parish events, making time to answer questions or talk with them about their experiences afterward.

If he/she says no, follow up with a question such as:

- What obstacles are keeping you from saying "yes"?

    Would you like to pray that these obstacles be removed; or

    Could I help you, | ne that can help you with these challenges?

- Is there anything else I could do to help you at this time? Is there someone else you would like to speak with?

DO NOT TAKE A "NO" ANSWER AS A FAILURE ON YOUR PART. It may be that they need to hear Jesus' invitation many times before they can respond with a "yes". God may have just needed you to be his instrument, at this time, to openly propose the possibility. You, or another person, may well be part of a subsequent conversation, after he/she has time to think about the possibility, where the answer will be quite different!

A CONVERSATION WITH DANIEL

Part One:

What thresholds do you hear in Daniel's story in Part One?

What actions or details from his story lead you to draw that conclusion?

If you were Daniel's friend, what questions might you ask him at this point?

If Daniel were to appear at your parish at this point in his story, what could the parish offer him? Is there something the parish should consider to help someone like Daniel at this point of the story?

Part Two:

What thresholds do you hear in Daniel's story in Part Two?

What actions or details from his story lead you to draw that conclusion?

If you were Daniel's friend, what questions might you ask him at this point?

If Daniel were to appear at your parish at this point in his story, what could the parish offer him? Is there something the parish should consider to help someone like Daniel at this point of the story?

Part Three:

At what thresholds do you hear in Daniel's story in Part Three?

What actions or details from his story lead you to draw that conclusion?

If you were Daniel's friend, what questions might you ask him at this point?

If Daniel were to appear at your parish at this point in his story, what could the parish offer him?

Is there something the parish should consider in order to help someone like Daniel at this point of the story?

SOME POINTS TO KEEP IN MIND:

- Daniel is telling his story from the perspective of being a disciple today.

- Listen for clues in the **story** in order to determine what threshold Daniel was at, **at that time.**

- How passive, or active, Daniel was in the story are significant clues that may help you identify the threshold. Recall that Catholics often confuse the passive threshold of openness with actively seeking.

- The breaks in the story do not necessarily coincide with the thresholds of conversion.

Part Four:

What thresholds do you hear in Daniel's story in Part Four?

What actions or details from his story lead you to draw that conclusion?

If you were Daniel's friend, what questions might you ask him at this point?

If Daniel were to appear at your parish at this point in his story, what could the parish offer him? Is there something the parish should consider to help someone like Daniel at this point of the story?

Part Five:

What thresholds do you hear in Daniel's story in Part Five?

What actions or details from his story lead you to draw that conclusion?

If you were Daniel's friend, what questions might you ask him at this point?

If Daniel were to appear at your parish at this point in his story, what could the parish offer him? Is there something the parish should consider to help someone like Daniel at this point of the story?

What Would You Say?

Take a moment to reflect again upon the person who came to mind during the opening prayer.

Based upon what you have learned thus far, where might a threshold conversation with this person begin? What might you need to be an effective guide for this person in the conversation?

Jot down your thoughts here:

Closing Prayer

"Who do you say that I am?"
– Luke 9:18-21

OPENING PRAYER

Follow these simple steps for your opening prayer:

1. Say a brief prayer. Invite the Holy Spirit to open your eyes and ears to what God has to say to you today through His Word.

2. One person reads the passage aloud. Allow for a moment of silence after the reading is complete.

3. Make note of any word or phrase that stands out to you in this passage.

4. As another person reads the passage, listen for your chosen word or phrase.

5. Say a prayer of gratitude to God for his presence in his Living Word you encountered in this moment.

6. Share with your partner(s) what stood out for you in this passage.

INTRODUCTION

Why know the *kerygma* — aka, **The Great Story of Jesus**?

The word, *kerygma* (kə-´erig-mə) is a Greek word that literally means "preaching" or "proclamation." The Great Story of Jesus: why he came, how he came, his life, his death, his resurrection and ascension, and his invitation for each and every man and woman to encounter him in order to make the choice to follow him in the midst of his Church, is the content of that proclamation.

"Being Christian is not the result of an ethical choice or a lofty idea, but the encounter with an event, a person, which gives life a new horizon and a decisive direction."

– Pope Emeritus Benedict XVI, Deus Caritas Est, 1, 2005

The *kerygma* we proclaim today

"The preaching of the early Church was centered on the proclamation of Jesus Christ, with whom the kingdom was identified. Now, as then, there is a need to unite the proclamation of the kingdom of God (the content of Jesus' own "kerygma") and the proclamation of the Christ-event (the "kerygma" of the apostles). The two proclamations are complementary; each throws light on the other. "

– St. John Paul II, Redemptoris Missio, 16

ACT ONE: THE KINGDOM

This means that all of creation, in the end, is conceived of to create the place of encounter between God and his creature—a place where the history of love between God and his creature can develop." – Benedict XVI, Pope Emeritus, October 6, 2008

"The kingdom of God is at hand." — Mark 1:15

Matthew 5:1-12	Mark 12:28-34	Matthew 13:31-32
Luke 1:50-54	Matthew 13:33	Romans 14:17

ACT TWO: JESUS, FACE OF THE KINGDOM

This means that all of creation, in the end, is conceived of to create the place of encounter between God and his creature—a place where the history of love between God and his creature can develop."

"[The] kingdom shone out before men in the word, in the works, and in the presence of Christ." – *Lumen Gentium*, 5

"The kingdom of God is not a concept, a doctrine, or a program subject to free interpretation, but it is before all else a person with the face and name of Jesus of Nazareth, the image of the invisible God." – Pope John Paul II, *Redemptoris Missio*, 18.

"And the Word became flesh and made his dwelling among us, and we saw his glory, the glory as of the Father's only Son, full of grace and truth." (John 1:14)

Matthew 1:21-23	*Mark 1:21-27*	*Luke 2:25-32*
Matthew 2:1-6	*Mark 3:11-12*	*Luke 4:16-21*
Matthew 8:23-27	*Mark 6:1-3*	*John 14:6*

ACT THREE: JESUS, THE KINGDOM IN WORD AND DEED

And [Jesus] said to them in reply, "Go and tell John what you have seen and heard: the blind regain their sight, the lame walk, lepers are cleansed, the deaf hear, the dead are raised, the poor have the good news proclaimed to them."
—Luke 7:22

"In [the Beatitudes] is all the novelty brought by Christ, and the whole novelty of Christ is in these words. In fact, the Beatitudes are Jesus' portrait, his way of life, and they are the way of true happiness, which we also can live with the grace Jesus gives us."
—Pope Francis, Wednesday Audience, August 7, 2014

Matthew 8:1-4	*Mark 4:1-20*	*Luke 5:17-26*	*John 2:1-12*
Matthew 8:5-13	*Mark 4:35-41*	*Luke 11:1-13*	*John 4:4-42*
Matthew 8:28-34	*Mark 5:21-34*	*Luke 7:21-23*	*John 9:1-11*
Matthew 9:1-8	*Mark 9:33-37*	*Luke 7:36-50*	*John 11:1-44*

and many, many more!

For Your Reflection —

1. Say a brief prayer, asking Jesus to join you as you read and pray his Word.

2. Choose one of the suggested scripture passages from **Acts Two** or **Three** of **The Great Story of Jesus.**

3. Read the passage you chose. If you can, without disturbing others, read it aloud, slowly, listening to every word.

4. Are there words or a phrase that stick out for you? Write those down here:

. . . .

. . . .

. . . .

5. Read the words again, paying particular attention to the words or phrases that caught your attention.

6. Read the passage one more time, this time imagining that Jesus is sitting with you as you read.

7. Share with Jesus what is in your mind and heart:

8. When you are done, say a prayer to Jesus, thanking him for this time. Or, you can say a "Glory Be to the Father…"

Are you in need of the healing touch of Jesus?

Or someone you know?

As you return to your place, write a name or the need on a slip of paper provided, fold it, and place it in the container in the prayer space. Your prayer offering will not be read by anyone. All slips will be destroyed unread at the end of the retreat.

ACT FOUR: JESUS EMBRACES THE CROSS

The Cross is not an ornament that we must always put in the churches, there on the altar. It is not a symbol that distinguishes us from others. The Cross is mystery, the mystery of God who humbles himself, he becomes 'nothing.' —Pope Francis, August 4, 2014

The cross is the unique sacrifice of Christ, the "one mediator between God and men." But because in his incarnate divine person he had in some way united himself to every man, "the possibility of being made partners, in a ways known to God, in the paschal mystery" is offered to all men. —*Catechism of the Catholic Church*, 619

"Apart from the cross, there is no other ladder by which we may get to heaven." — St. Rose of Lima

"When my goodness saw that you could be drawn in no other way, I sent him to be lifted onto the wood of the cross. I made of that cross an anvil where this child of humankind could be hammered into an instrument to release humankind from death and restore it to the life of grace. In this way he drew everything to himself: for he proved his unspeakable love, and the human heart is always drawn by love."
—St. Catherine of Siena, *The Dialogue*

Matthew 20:28	*John 10:17-18*	*Colossians 2:13-15*
Mark 8:31	*John 3:17*	*Philippians 2:6-11*
1 Corinthians 1:18-25		*2 Timothy 2:5*

A Reflection on the Cross —

Find a quiet place where you can see the cross.

After you have settled in, say a brief prayer, asking Jesus to join you in your meditation.

Gaze upon the cross. Imagine you are there with Jesus, Mary and Mary Magdalene. You may find one of these Scripture passages a helpful guide to your meditation.

Matthew 27:33-56 *John 19: 16-30* *1 Corinthians 1:18-25* *Philippians 2:5-11*

What do you hear? See? Smell? Feel? What do you want to say to Jesus?

Record your thoughts here:

. . . .

. . . .

. . . .

. . . .

. . . .

ACT FIVE: RESURRECTION AND ASCENSION

I am the resurrection and the life; whoever believes in me, even if he dies, will live, and everyone who lives and believes in me will never die. Do you believe this?"—John 11:25-26

"For I handed on to you as of first importance what I also received: that Christ died for our sins in accordance with the scriptures; that he was buried; that he was raised on the third day in accordance with the scriptures; that he appeared to Cephas, and then to the Twelve." —1 Corinthians 15:3-4

Matthew 28:1-10   *Mark 16:1-20*   *Luke 24:1-12*

Luke 24:14-35   *John 20:1-23*   *Acts 1:6-12*   *Acts 2:29-36*

Why does it matter Jesus rose from the dead?

What does that mean for you?

ACT FIVE/PART 2: THE HOLY SPIRIT

God's love has been poured into our hearts through the Holy Spirit who has been given to us. – **Romans 5:5**

"Holy Spirit, come into my heart, and in your power draw it to you." —St. Catherine of Siena

"I will ask the Father, and he will give you another Advocate to be with you always …The Advocate, the Holy Spirit that the Father will send in my name—he will teacher you everything and remind you of all that [I] told you." – John 14: 16, 26

Genesis 1:2   *Isaiah 11:1-2*   *Ezekiel 36:26-27*   *Matthew 3:11-12*   *Matthew 28:18-20*
Mark 1:9-11   *Luke 4:16-21*   *John 14:15-26*   *John 20:21-23*   *Acts 1:8*
Acts 2:1-13   *Acts 2:38*   *Romans 5:1-5*   *Romans 8:2-6*   *Romans 8:26-27*
1 Corinthians 2:9-10

What did you hear about the Holy Spirit that intrigued you?
What would the presence of the Holy Spirit mean for you now, in your life?

Take some time now to reflect upon these first five acts of The Great Story of Jesus.

1. Was there one act you found familiar and/or comforting?

2. Was there one act you found particularly challenging?

3. Was there one you have more questions than answers about?

4. Which one are you drawn to spend time with right now?

You may use this space to write down your thoughts.

ACT SIX: JESUS ASKS ME TO FOLLOW HIM

In all of his life Jesus presents himself as our model. He is 'the perfect man,' who invites us to become his disciples and follow him. In humbling himself, he has given us an example to imitate, through his prayer he draws us to pray, and by his poverty he calls us to accept freely the privation and persecutions that may come our way."

— *Catechism of the Catholic Church*, 520

"As Jesus passed on from there, he saw a man named Matthew sitting at the customs post. He said to him, 'Follow me.' And he got up and followed him." — Matthew 9:9

"And [Jesus] said to them, 'Follow me, and I will make you fishers of men.' — Matthew 4:18

Matthew 4:18-20   **Luke 5:1-11**   **Mark 1:16-19**
Matthew 9:9-13   **John 1:35-51**

Have I heard the invitation of Jesus to "Follow me"? How have I responded?

ACT SEVEN: PERSONAL SIN AND FORGIVENESS

What obstacle, sin or attachment stands between you and Jesus?

They signaled to their partners in the other boat to come to help them. They came and filled both boats so that they were in danger of sinking. When Simon Peter saw this, he fell at the knees of Jesus and said, "Depart from me, Lord, for I am a sinful man." —Luke 5:7-8

"Then Jesus straightened up and said to her, 'Woman, where are they? Has no one condemned you?' She replied, 'No one, sir.' Then Jesus said, 'Neither do I condemn you. Go, and from now on do not sin any more.'" —John 8:10-11

"Jesus came to "free men from the gravest slavery, sin, which thwarts them in their vocation as God's sons (and daughters) and causes all kinds of human bondage."

—*Catechism of the Catholic Church*, 549

Luke 5:3-8   **Luke 24:46-47**   **1 John 1:8**

ACT EIGHT: JESUS' INVITATION – NEW LIFE BY ADOPTION

But when the fullness of time had come, God sent his Son, born of a woman, born under the law, to ransom those under the law, so that we might receive adoption. As proof that you are children, God sent the spirit of his Son into our hearts, crying out, 'Abba, Father!' So you are no longer a slave but a child, and if a child then also an heir, through God.
—Galatians 4:4-7

John 1:12-13　　　*Romans 6:3-4*　　　*1 Corinthians 15:22*
2 Corinthians 5:17　*2 Corinthians 6:18*　*Ephesians 1:4-6*
Colossians 1:18

What does it mean that God the Father chose *you*? That you are His adopted son/daughter?

· ·

· ·

· ·

· ·

ACT EIGHT: JESUS' INVITATION – BE MY DISCIPLE

At once they left their nets and followed him."
—Matthew 4:20

"Let this be thy whole endeavor, this thy prayer, this thy desire – that thou mayest be stripped of all selfishness, and with entire simplicity follow Jesus only."
—Thomas à Kempis, *Imitation of Christ*

"No one can say 'Jesus is Lord' except by the Holy Spirit."
—1 Corinthians 12:3

Matthew 16:13-17　　*Mark 10:46-52*　　*Acts 8:26-39*
Acts 9:1-19　　　　*Acts 10:44-48*

Have I already dropped my nets?
If I am not quite ready to do so, what could help me drop my nets?

· ·

· ·

· ·

· ·

ACT EIGHT: JESUS' INVITATION –
BE PART OF MY BODY, THE CHURCH

"The one mediator, Christ, established and ever sustains here on earth his holy Church, the community of faith, of hope, and charity, as a visible organization through which he communicates truth and grace to all." — *Lumen Gentium* 8

"Now you are Christ's body, and individually parts of it." — 1 Corinthians 12:27

"He is the head of the body, the church." — Colossians 1:18

"I am the vine, you are the branches. Whoever remains in me and I in him will bear much fruit, because without me you can do nothing." — John 15:5

Matthew 18:20	*Matthew 28:18-20*	*John 13:34*	*Acts 1:13-14*
Acts 2:1-13	*Acts 2:42-47*	*Acts 4:32-35*	*Romans 12*
1 Corinthians 12	*Galatians 3:26-29*	*Ephesians 4*	*Colossians 1:15-20*
Colossians 1:24-29	*Colossians 3:12-17*	*1 Thessalonians 5:12-22*	
Hebrews 10:19-25	*1 Peter 2*		

How have I responded to Jesus' invitation to become part of his Body, the Church?

Is Jesus inviting me to renew my commitment to be part of his Body?

ACT NINE: LIFE OF DISCIPLESHIP

Following Jesus...

Being a disciple means being constantly ready to bring the love of Jesus to others, and this can happen unexpectedly and in any place: on the street, in a city square, during work, on a journey." —Pope Francis, *Evangelii Gaudium*, 127

"Just so, your light must shine before others, that they may see your good deeds and glorify your heavenly Father."
—Matthew 5:16

"Go therefore and make disciples of all nations." —Matthew 28:19

Matthew 16:24-25	*Matthew 25:34-40*	*Luke 3:10-14*	*John 13:34-35*
John 15:5	*Acts 2:42-47*	*1 Corinthians 12:12-31*	

For Your Reflection –

Review your notes on the Great Story of Jesus. What part of the story moved you the most?

Recall that experience now. Remember it could have been a memory, or an emotion, or an image. What is the message Jesus has for you this day? You may use this page to record your thoughts:

. . . .

. . . .

. . . .

. . . .

. . . .

. . . .

. . . .

. . . .

. . . .

. . . .

. . . .

. . . .

. . . .

. . . .

. . . .

. . . .

DO TELL: SHARING YOUR STORY

Opening Prayer
Lectio Divina:
The Samaritan Woman tells *her* story

Instructions are found on page 57 of this manual.

The woman left her water jar and went into the town and said to the people, "Come see a man who told me everything I have done. Could he possibly be the Messiah?" They went out of the town and came to him ...

Many of the Samaritans of that town began to believe in him because of the word of the woman* who testified, "He told me everything I have done."

When the Samaritans came to him, they invited him to stay with them; and he stayed there two days.

Many more began to believe in him because of his word, and they said to the woman, "We no longer believe because of your word; for we have heard for ourselves, and we know that this is truly the savior of the world

.—**John 4: 28-30; 39-42**

She tells the people of the village about *her* encounter with Jesus.

Ask the Holy Spirit to bring to mind someone you love (it could be: family, friend, neighbor, co-worker) who needs to hear how you met Jesus. It doesn't have to be the first time you encountered Jesus, or the last time you encountered Jesus.

As you think about the person who has come to mind, what "Jesus story" of yours could you share?

Telling Your Story

Think about your friend...
...does he or she trust you enough to listen to your story of coming to know Jesus?

The goal of sharing your story: that your friend will take at least one step closer to Jesus.

WHAT YOU SHARE:

The difference being close to Jesus has made in your life;

> *What your life was like before this particular encounter with Jesus;*
> *What happened during this encounter;*
> *What helped you move closer;*
> *How your life was different after this encounter.*

WHAT DO I SAY?

To figure out what to say, it often helps to first consider what NOT to say.
Do not overwhelm your friend with a five-gallon story when a thimbleful is necessary!
We are rarely expected to share our whole conversion story in one sitting—rather, we share one piece of our story that seems to be what they need at this time, in this place.

HOW DO I KNOW WHERE TO START?

Begin with this question:

- What spiritual threshold do I think my friend is at right now?

Knowing where a person in their lived relationship with God is a vital clue to knowing where to start in sharing your story.

Remember! We share our story to help our friend take the next step in their relationship with Jesus.

If you think your friend is at trust, what part of your story could arouse curiosity about Jesus?

Think about a time when your curiosity was aroused:

- Was it something someone did, or said?
- Something you saw, or perhaps heard or read?
- Perhaps was it an answered prayer?
- What difference did your curiosity make in your life—did it bring you peace?
- Did it unsettle you? or increase in you a desire to know more about Jesus?
- What did you do then?

If you think your friend is at curiosity, how could your story open for them the possibility of a relationship with Jesus (recall: openness comes with an openness to a possibility of change?)

Think about a time when you became open to the possibility of a relationship with Jesus:

- What moved *you* to consider a relationship with Jesus *for yourself?*
- Was there a catalyst that moved you into openness (life changing event, a book you read, movie you saw, that moved you to consider the possibility of making a change in your life, to make room for Jesus)?
- What kind of changes did you contemplate in your life? Was it scary to consider?
- Recall that defenses are high between curiosity and openness: being honest about the challenges of being open to a relationship with Jesus, especially the feeling of loss of control, can be very helpful for people.

- When you found you could be open to the possibility, what happened next? Did you desire to become closer to Jesus? Did you back away for a while? Did you find you crossed this threshold more than once?

- Who were your friends in this crazy time? How did they help you?

- How did prayer sustain you during this period of your life? What kinds of prayer helped you move closer to Jesus?

If you think your friend is at openness, how could your story open for them the possibility of actively seeking a relationship with Jesus?

Think of when you moved from thinking about the possibility of a relationship with Jesus to actively seeking that relationship for yourself:

- What kicked you into actively seeking Jesus vs. mentally thinking about the possibility?

- Did you have an "Ananias" walking with you then? What did they say or do that helped you seek Jesus?

- With seeking often comes an awareness of personal sin. How did that awareness move you to repentance and change?

- How did your prayer life change? Were there others praying for you? What were you praying for?

- Was there something you read, a video or podcast you heard, that helped you then?

- Was there a person's story, a life of a saint that helped you at this stage in your journey?

- What were your obstacles to saying "yes" to Jesus? What helped you remove the obstacles: prayer, spiritual conversations, celebration of the sacrament of reconciliation?

If you think your friend is on the verge of intentional discipleship, what is your story of saying "yes" to God?

Realize that many of us make the journey through the thresholds more than once. Focus on the one time you said "yes" to God — sharing the one that you think will help your friend the most right now:

Remember what it was like to stand on the edge of your "yes".

- Do you recall the experience of spiritual forces tempting you to walk away from Jesus? What was that like?

- What were your fears about saying yes?

- What was your greatest desire you hoped to gain from your yes?

- What was it like in those early weeks after you said yes, to walk as an intentional disciple?

- Who were your friends who helped you say yes? How did they support you and help you to shun the temptation to go back to your old life?

To Identify Where to Start

- What have you talked about in the past?

- What desires or hopes have they shared with you?

- What has been your conversations in the past about God? Jesus? Church?

- Did they ask you specific questions?

- What spiritual threshold do you think they are at, at this moment in time?

Note: This is not an exact science but a best guess to identify a place to start in sharing your story.

- Can you describe the moment when you said yes to Jesus?

- Who was there to help you in that moment?

- Describe the fruits of your walk with the Lord. What helps you stay close to Jesus?

PRACTICE TELLING YOUR STORY

Share your story as you would share it with your friend.

Do not reveal the identity of your friend—just describe at what threshold you think he/she is right now.

After you share your story, the others in your group will ask questions, to help you clarify the details of your story—they may even notice something you missed in your own story!

You will have the opportunity to do the same for each person in the group.

CLOSING PRAYER: "LOOK UP AND SEE"

Preparation:

In the story of the Samaritan woman and Jesus, when the disciples return to find the two in conversation, Jesus challenges them to "look up and see the fields ripe for the harvest" for the woman is returning to the well with her fellow villagers.

Jesus also challenges us to "look up and see" those around us in need of his redeeming love and mercy.

Ask Jesus to help you see those he wants you to see: who comes to mind? Write their names on your slip of paper.

- What grace do you ask from Jesus, to help you be Ananias to those you see?
- Write that on the other side of your paper.

When you return home, you may want to find a special place to keep it, so that you can refer to it occasionally.

[Sign of the Cross]

Lord Jesus,

We thank you for the privilege to be an Ananias for you in our world. May we stay close to you in humble service, to bring others closer to you.

Holy Spirit,

We ask for the grace to be open to your presence and your gifts.

May the gift of courage embolden us to respond to Jesus' command to "look up and see";

May the gift of understanding enable us to see beyond our fears and preconceptions to the per-son to whom we are sent, created in the Father's image;

May the gift of knowledge equip us to know stories to tell;

May the gift of wisdom enable us to know when to tell stories … and when to listen;
May the gift of counsel equip us to ask the right questions … at the right time;

May the gift of reverence remind us to give glory and praise to you for the work you do through us;

May the gift of fear of the Lord help us to marvel at the work of your hands and heart in us and through us.

And may all these gifts strengthen us and prepare us to use our charisms to be the unique Ananias we are called to be in this world.

We ask all these things in the most Holy Name of Jesus.
Amen.

APPENDIX 1: LECTIO DIVINA "DIVINE READING"

One of the most beautiful ways for entering into prayer is through the Word of God. Lectio divina brings you into direct conversation with the Lord and it opens for you wisdom's treasure. The intimate friendship with the One who loves us, enables us to see with the eyes of God, to speak with his Word in our hearts, to treasure the beauty of that experience and to share it with those who are hungry for eternity.

— Pope Francis, "Letter to the Carmelites on the Occasion of the General Chapter 2013"

Lectio Divina is a very ancient art of prayer through Scripture that traces its origins to the Desert Fathers. It found its way first into monastic life and it continues to this day among Catholics from every walk of life as part of their daily prayer, either in groups or alone.

There are four parts of the prayer in classic Lectio Divina:

LECTIO - A Scripture passage is read gently and slowly, constantly listening for the "still, small voice" of God: in a word or phrase that somehow speaks to the person.

MEDITATIO - The passage is read again. This time, reflecting on the text of the passage and thinking about how it applies to one's own life.

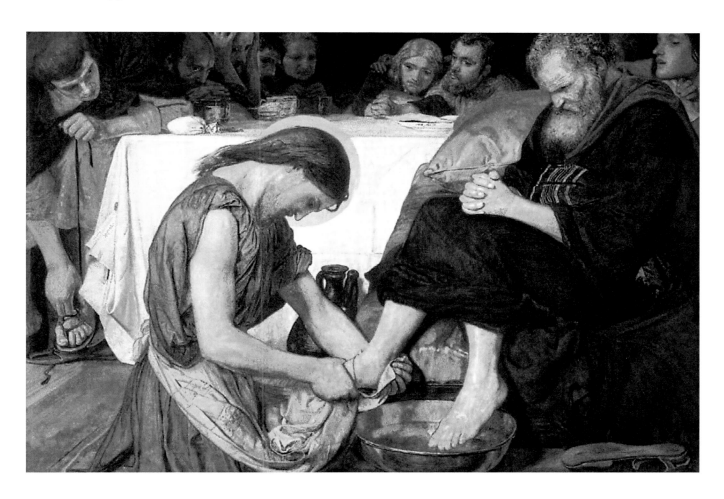

ORATIO – After reading it a third time, the person speaks to God by opening their heart. This is not primarily an intellectual exercise, but is more the beginning of a conversation with God.

CONTEMPLATIO - "Speak, Lord. Your servant is listening." This is a freeing of oneself from one's own thoughts, both mundane and holy, listening for God's voice with the "ears of the heart."

Lectio Divina: Step-by-Step

For our purposes, we will be using the following steps:

First, say a brief prayer, asking God to open your mind and heart to the words of Scripture. **Next**, slowly, prayerfully, read the chosen passage. Listen, "with the ears of your heart." What memory or image does the passage stir up inside you?

Does an event from the past week surface here? Record those on the pages provided, or in a notebook.

Then, read the passage again, listening for those words that strike you. What does this passage say to you now?

Now, read the passage, slowly, prayerfully, a third time. You may also wish to imagine yourself in the scene, or actually hearing these words from Jesus.

Listen to what God has to say to **you.** Are these words of consolation, challenge, or both? Or perhaps they have some other impact on you. What is it?

Finally, say a prayer of thanksgiving to God for this time with Him. A simple "Glory Be" is sufficient, if you wish.

> *The process, whether you are praying the Scriptures alone, in a small group, or with a partner, is the same. In each situation, try to find a quiet place where you are not distracted. Turn off the radio, your cell phone, or anything else that is a distraction. Follow each step of the process. Do not rush, take your time.*

Lectio Divina alone

- Speak the Word of God aloud, if you are able. Let the Word seep into your spirit, through not only your eyes but your ears, as well.

- *You may find journaling a big help to your solitary prayer. After several weeks, or a month, look back and see how your prayer has changed… and how it has changed you!*

Lectio Divina in a small group

- If your group is larger than six, split into small groups of no more than five, no less than three, members.

- Have a different person read the passage each time. Hold all discussion until the end of the process.

- Do not be afraid of silence. Be open to hearing the "still, small voice" of God to be found in moments of silence.

- *Keep in mind this old adage: God gave us two ears and one mouth. It may be God's way of saying listen at least twice as much as we talk!*

Lectio Divina with a partner

- Take turns reading the passage. Take the time to reflect upon the questions after each reading. Hold your discussion until the end of the process.

- Do not be afraid of silence. Be open to hearing the "still, small voice" of God to be found in moments of silence.

Note: *Some people add a fifth step: Actio. This is especially common with small groups that meet on a regular basis. During this step, each person reflects silently on this question: Does this passage, your response, and your time with the Lord call you to action in the coming week? Each person may wish to record any thoughts you might have in this regard. Some groups begin their next meeting by sharing the week's experience in light of this prayer.*

Appendix 2: Threshold Conversation Chart

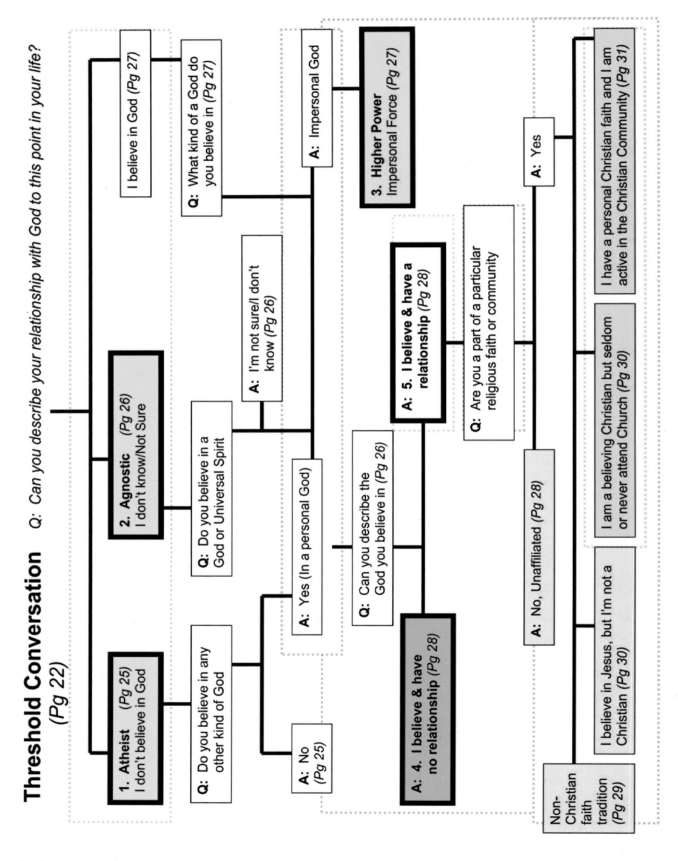

Threshold Conversation Q: *Can you describe your relationship with God to this point in your life?* *(Pg 22)*

I believe in God *(Pg 27)*

Q: What kind of a God do you believe in *(Pg 27)*

A: Impersonal God

3. Higher Power Impersonal Force *(Pg 27)*

2. Agnostic *(Pg 26)* I don't know/Not Sure

Q: Do you believe in a God or Universal Spirit

A: I'm not sure/I don't know *(Pg 26)*

A: Yes (In a personal God)

Q: Can you describe the God you believe in *(Pg 26)*

A: 5. I believe & have a relationship *(Pg 28)*

Q: Are you a part of a particular religious faith or community

A: Yes

I have a personal Christian faith and I am active in the Christian Community *(Pg 31)*

1. Atheist *(Pg 25)* I don't believe in God

Q: Do you believe in any other kind of God

A: No *(Pg 25)*

A: 4. I believe & have no relationship *(Pg 28)*

A: No, Unaffiliated *(Pg 28)*

I am a believing Christian but seldom or never attend Church *(Pg 30)*

I believe in Jesus, but I'm not a Christian *(Pg 30)*

Non-Christian faith tradition *(Pg 29)*